Poetry Wonderland

Cumbria & County Durham

Edited By Jenni Harrison

First published in Great Britain in 2019 by:

Young Writers
Remus House
Coltsfoot Drive
Peterborough
PE2 9BF
Telephone: 01733 890066
Website: www.youngwriters.co.uk

All Rights Reserved
Book Design by Spencer Hart
© Copyright Contributors 2019
SB ISBN 978-1-78988-598-9
Printed and bound in the UK by BookPrintingUK
Website: www.bookprintinguk.com
YB0406U

FOREWORD

Here at Young Writers, we love to let imaginations run wild and creativity go crazy. Our aim is to encourage young people to get their creative juices flowing and put pen to paper. Each competition is tailored to the relevant age group, hopefully giving each pupil the inspiration and incentive to create their own piece of creative writing, whether it's a poem or a short story. By allowing them to see their own work in print, we know their confidence and love for the written word will grow.

For our latest competition Poetry Wonderland, we invited primary school pupils to create wild and wonderful poems on any topic they liked – the only limits were the limits of their imagination! Using poetry as their magic wand, these young poets have conjured up worlds, creatures and situations that will amaze and astound or scare and startle! Using a variety of poetic forms of their own choosing, they have allowed us to get a glimpse into their vivid imaginations. We hope you enjoy wandering through the wonders of this book as much as we have.

CONTENTS

The Poems

My Picnic On The Moon

My cat and I went for a trip
To the moon to have a little picnic,
Our rocket landed before noon
On the far side of the moon.
We laid out our blanket and food,
Tom, my cat, said, "Let's eat dude!"
But our picnic did not go to plan,
There was moon dust in the cheese flan!
My jelly wibbled and wobbled and floated away,
Our juice poured out the opposite way.
Tom said, "Let's have some fun!"
So we played a game in the sun.
But our Frisbee soared away, fast like a rocket
And a little green head popped out and said,
"I'll have this!" and put it in his pocket!

Ellie Jane Boyes (8)
Appleby Primary School, Appleby-In-Westmorland

Funny Football

F un football we all like to play,
U nder the crossbar makes our day!
N ow and again we go upside down,
N ot again, the fans will frown,
Y ikes, we'd better spin it back around.

F ootball is the greatest game,
"O ver here!" said James,
O oohh so close!
T he fans are on their feet,
B ig shot in the top corner,
A goal for team Funny,
L egs are losing, the whistle blows,
L aughs and cheers from team Funny!

Champions!

James Park (8)
Appleby Primary School, Appleby-In-Westmorland

Tooth Fairy For Tea

Today is the day the Tooth Fairy is coming,
I have been baking since Tuesday night,
Here is a list of the things I have made
That I hope she will like:

Popcorn sandwiches,
Chicken lollipops,
Sausage cupcakes,
Peanut butter and chocolate dip,
Milk teeth breadcrumbs,
Glitter and jam crackers,
Apple and blueberry milkshake!

The Tooth Fairy and I had a lovely time,
We giggled and laughed so much,
I hope she comes back for another visit,
Until then I will dream of the day
The Tooth Fairy came for tea!

Hannah Robinson (7)
Appleby Primary School, Appleby-In-Westmorland

Cupcake Crazy

There was a cupcake
Who wanted a friend,
So one day he said,
"Let's bake a cake and mend!"

Out came the ingredients
Of sugar, eggs and flour,
It only took an hour,
He fussed and he quizzed,
He mixed and he whizzed,
He messed and he slopped
Until he had mopped.
Into the oven he goes,
Until it was time,
Then, *ding-a-ling!*
With a little ping
He pops out of the oven like a king!
With all sorts of buttons and chocolate too,
A cupcake poo,
Who was crazy too!

Ashlyn Robinson (8)
Appleby Primary School, Appleby-In-Westmorland

Toilets Fly

T o all toilet flights, the only food you eat is
O nions, because then you can fly!
I gloos are needed to sleep,
L egs won't be needed because you can fly,
E nergy is needed to fly as high as a kite,
T ango dancing is not allowed,
S inging is essential,

F lying might run out, so eat more onions,
L ovely toilets get to be VIP,
Y et again, toilets fly!

Gracie Dakin (8)
Appleby Primary School, Appleby-In-Westmorland

Giant Wonderland

I tried to get to Giant Wonderland,
I tried and tried,
I never gave up,
But when the rain came down
There was nowhere else to stay,
Then, I found a toilet,
I trained it very well,
It became my pet,
I love it very much,
We finally got to Giant Wonderland,
Oh, what a beautiful sight,
Then we saw a tremendous giant,
We ran and ran until we got home.

Jane Teasdale (8)
Appleby Primary School, Appleby-In-Westmorland

Candy Land

If I lived in a land of candy I could...

Sail down a chocolate river
On a boat made from Matchmakers and Mars Bars,
Sledge down a marshmallow mountain
On a candy cane sledge,
Go to a gummy bear wedding
And watch them kiss
Under a Love Heart sunset,
Eat a gingerbread house
With a cola bottle to drink,
Or do a chewing gum bungee jump!

Liam Marshall (9)
Appleby Primary School, Appleby-In-Westmorland

Football On The Moon

The day came, we played football on the moon,
We got to our rocket just after noon,
The referee blew his little tune.
Today's match was Alien Utd vs Hogwarts FC,
All the crowd got in for free
Because there was no security.
The ball bounced high because there was no gravity,
Would you believe, the final score was four-three?

Luke Lightfoot (7)
Appleby Primary School, Appleby-In-Westmorland

Burger Land

Aliens, aliens everywhere,
Looking for burgers down below,
To Earth we go, ahoy, let's go!
We landed safe and sound above ground,
We scuttled and ran above the land
To find Burger Land,
We smelt the meat,
We dove and pushed
As we had to scoff as much as possible
And off we go to Planet Yo!
Bye!

Jenson Brennan (8)
Appleby Primary School, Appleby-In-Westmorland

Walking On The Moon

The spoon walked on the moon,
And sang a little tune,
The knife brought his wife,
And had a good life,
The plate brought his mate,
And ate some food,
And, well, the fork ate some pork,
When the fork ate his pork,
He saw a space rocket,
And the space rocket was blue with lots of goo!

Lexie Mae Park (9)
Appleby Primary School, Appleby-In-Westmorland

Spam

My son looks like a cream bun,
Legs like jelly, hair like jam,
His favourite food is Spam!
Spam for breakfast,
Spam for brunch,
Even Spam for Christmas lunch!
Spam on toast, jellied Spam,
Spam Bolognese instead of ham,
My son looks like a cream bun!

Caleb Mahoney (8)
Appleby Primary School, Appleby-In-Westmorland

The Amazing Animals

There was once a cow with a spoon,
Who realised it was noon,
So they went to the moon
To find a tomato in a balloon.

Chloe Thwaites (8)
Appleby Primary School, Appleby-In-Westmorland

An Underwater Carnival

I got in a strange invention at a carnival under the sea,
I got in a submarine to see what it could be,
I saw sharks with lasers swimming through fire hoops,
Next, there were hundreds of colourful clownfish doing loop-the-loops!
A raft floated by with singing starfish and music playing,
With seahorses singing as loud as they could,
A clown octopus spinning coral plates and juggling seaweed balls
Came past, he was very good,
I swam out of the submarine to get a better look,
A crab waddled over to me and gave me a joke book,
I found a gap in the coral to hide from the terrifying, floating water snake,
He was just about to eat and then I felt a shake,
"Wake up Charlie!" Phew, it was all a dream!

Charlie Gribble (9)
Flookburgh CE Primary School, Flookburgh

The World Of Candyfloss

I went to the playground
And I saw a massive hole in the ground,
So, I jumped in and there was...
Candyfloss Land!
I thought my feet were stuck in some sand,
But then, to my surprise
I had candy in my hand.
As I started to walk
The candyfloss trees began to talk,
"Eat me! Eat me!" they shouted.
I bit into the tree
And there was candy as far as I could see,
Some birds flew past with candyfloss wings
And said, "Careful how much you pick, you don't want to be sick!"
So I stopped eating, then I ran into Candyfloss Town
And I bought lots of candy and candyfloss!

Jacob Luke Burrow (9)
Flookburgh CE Primary School, Flookburgh

The One-Eyed Scare

There are rumours about
A monster so foul
That lives in a cave underground.

It's evil and tall
With a deep-throated roar
And smells of rotten old flesh.

A single large eye,
Sharp horns on its head
And vampire teeth that fill you with dread.

It had fur like a bear that can easily scare,
A long, scaly tail that follows behind
And only one leg. "From Bigfoot," they said.

Now, I'm big and strong,
I don't believe rumours this long,
But, what's that I can hear?
A thud on the stairs! Oh no! I think I'm done!

Seamus Atkinson (9)
Flookburgh CE Primary School, Flookburgh

The Invisible Door

The invisible door leads to some amazing places,
Upside-down worlds and strange-looking faces,
Weird creatures like caterpillars and dancing flamingos,
A world of cheese and candyfloss,
A forest of chocolate trees and mince pie rocks,
The invisible door has a cannon and a slide
To take you to places you can hide
With magical rainbows, snowy fields and sunny beaches,
The invisible door even takes you to magical lands like Hogwarts!
Where you can see Harry Potter, the greatest wizard of all!

Alfie Chapman (8)
Flookburgh CE Primary School, Flookburgh

Wonderful Clouds

Look, up there!
It's a cloud!
Look at it, shifting into shapes,
Maybe it'll turn into a grape!
It looks so high up, there in the sky,
I wish I could go up there,
Oh look, it turned into a pear!
Clouds can turn into lots of things
Like places, shapes, things that you use in everyday life
And even faces!
Imagine if the clouds went to the moon
In the afternoon!
I love clouds, you could jump on them
But not very loud!

Debra Njeri Nyamai (9)
Flookburgh CE Primary School, Flookburgh

Lego Adventures

Come on an adventure with me,
Let's jump into my Lego box and see
What we can build,
There are all sorts of colours
And all sorts of shapes,
We can stack and connect them
And see what we can create.
Dragons and pirate ships
And spaceships galore,
Come on an awesome adventure,
There is lots to explore,
Just be careful not to leave
Any Lego on the floor!

James McClure (8)
Flookburgh CE Primary School, Flookburgh

Dancing On Beans On Toast

Dancing on beans on toast,
Better than a chicken roast.
Dancing on strawberry jelly,
Better than eating a welly.
Dancing on tomato sauce,
You don't need lots of force.
Dancing on pickled onions,
Less painful than having bunions.
Dancing on a knickerbocker glory,
A fitting end to the story!

Holly Lloyd (8)
Flookburgh CE Primary School, Flookburgh

The Giant Floating Bubble

Whoosh! The wind blows me up into the light blue sky,
I can see the lush green fields below me,
Whoosh! It smells extremely soapy
And it feels light and floaty,
Whoosh! My bubble pops on a spiky tree branch,
Argh! I fall onto the muddy, spiky grass with a bump!

Lucie Isla Rowlandson (8)
Flookburgh CE Primary School, Flookburgh

The Dolphin

The dolphin swims in the deep blue sea,
Jumping into the waves as happy as can be,
Using his echo to find his tea,
Along came a group of fish,
The perfect dinner dish!
Better than he could wish,
With a full belly
He swims off to watch telly!

Amelia Roberts (8)
Flookburgh CE Primary School, Flookburgh

The Dancing Guinea Pigs

Freddie and Pipsy
Like to get tipsy
Dancing around in their hutch,
When they get fed
They should go to bed
But piggies prefer to stay up!
The moon comes out
And the stars shine bright,
So Freddie and Pipsy dance all night!

Louis Bennett (7)
Flookburgh CE Primary School, Flookburgh

Puppy Love

My puppy has no gloom,
His ears stick up like antlers,
He messes up my bedroom,
He eats my teddies, I don't know what to do,
My puppy never stops eating,
We're going to run out of food!

Niamh Nelson (8)
Flookburgh CE Primary School, Flookburgh

Kitty Cats

Kitty cats scream and scratch,
Then they like to chase the rats,
Kitty cats hate the bath,
Then they scream some more!

Mya Barton (8)
Flookburgh CE Primary School, Flookburgh

When I Jumped On A Cactus

When I jumped on a cactus,
I could smell the dusty, scratchy and stinky sand,
When I jumped on a cactus,
I could hear the cactus squeaking and the wind blowing horrendously,
When I jumped on a cactus,
I could taste the tasty, sticky juice from the cactus as well as the crunchy, disgusting sand,
When I jumped on a cactus,
I could see a storm that I made from the horrible sand,
When I jumped on a cactus,
I could feel the spiky, dangerous and terrifying spikes.

Nadia Marcinczak (8)
Hensingham Community Primary School, Hensingham

When I Jumped On A Cactus

I can smell the horrible fiery air all around me
I can hear a mysterious noise
I can touch some pointy spikes
I can see clumpy, scruffy and sprinkly sand
I can taste something spiky and it is green and horrible.

Evie Lister (8)
Hensingham Community Primary School, Hensingham

If I Were A Rabbit

If I were a rabbit,
I would see long wavy leaves,
I would smell beautiful, amazing flowers,
I would taste lots of astonishing carrots,
I would touch sharp, crispy grass.

Timothy Chadwick (7)
Hensingham Community Primary School, Hensingham

Living In A Winter Wonderland

W inter is coming and the elves are making presents,
I cicles freeze on the mountain top,
N obody is out because the weather is as cold as a freezer,
T oys are getting made as fast as lightning,
E lves are as tired as a towing tortoise,
R ainy every day and night.

W inter is the best time because you can have snowball fights,
O n snow Sunday we toast s'mores as the gloomy night goes down,
N ight falls as Santa comes to town,
D eer are playing in the snow, as elegant as swans,
E agles are flying through the sky as snow falls down,
R abbits run to their holes as snowflakes fall,
L ights on your roof as Santa comes to town,
A s winter comes, the snowy hail will fall,

N aughty people don't get any presents as they
have been bad,
D ownstairs there are piles of presents as you
walk through the door.

Sophie Leigh Crawford (9)
Holm Cultram Abbey CE Primary School, Abbeytown

The Minotaur, Burger And Professor Toy

The Minotaur is beastly,
As slithery as a snake,
He can crawl scarily like a spider,
The burger is as soft as a bed,
And as bouncy as a cloud.
Professor Toy is as clever as a pro
And as dumb as a rook.
The Minotaur lived in a gloomy cave,
Staring out on a bouncy sofa
As bouncy as a bouncy castle,
He wants more scary skulls to collect,
Like a bird with a worm, feeding the baby birds,
The bouncy sofa was as lumpy as a rock
And Professor Toy was as grumpy as a bear.

Leland Graham (8)
Holm Cultram Abbey CE Primary School, Abbeytown

The Waffle Jumping Into A Toaster

There lived a toasty, warm waffle,
As warm as a sausage,
The warm waffle saw a shiny toaster,
As clean as a frog,
The waffle bounced into the shiny toaster,
Then he popped out like a frog
Jumping off a lily pad,
He was so hot he jumped in the sink
Like a kangaroo,
But then a giant human came
And he was as big as the giant from Jack and the Beanstalk!
And then the waffle jumped into the giant's mouth,
As big as a hole.

Kaine Riddick (9)
Holm Cultram Abbey CE Primary School, Abbeytown

The Underwater Drag Race

Under the ocean, it was as dark as night,
As loud as thunder,
As scary as lightning,
The cars were as still as seaweed,
The fuel floated like balloons,
The drivers were frozen like ice
Because they all ran out of oxygen,
The lights blew up like grenades
Because of the water,
It was a disaster!

Connor Riddick (7)
Holm Cultram Abbey CE Primary School, Abbeytown

The Scary, Angry Gingerbread House!

The dark gingerbread house,
It was as slithery as a snake,
As grizzly as a grizzly bear,
As slimy as a ghost living in a bath,
As frightening as a monster jumping out of a bush,
As deadly as a deadly scorpion,
The house burnt down in flames.

Lexi Millar (8)
Holm Cultram Abbey CE Primary School, Abbeytown

Winter Wonderland

Winter is coming, nights freeze,
As icy as a freezer,
As light as snow,
As dark as night,
The trees are as cold as snow,
Santa is as happy as children,
The elves are busy putting the Christmas tree up.

Charlotte Wilson (8)
Holm Cultram Abbey CE Primary School, Abbeytown

Remember

As memorable as a puppy,
As thinkable as a Minotaur,
A cave as ugly as a monkey,
As thinkable as a scaly dragon,
As dreamy as a dog,
As un-dreamy as Medusa,
As sleepy as a mad gnome.

Theo Timperon (9)
Holm Cultram Abbey CE Primary School, Abbeytown

Bubblegum Land

Bubblegum Land is...

As red as a rose,
As bubbly as a bath,
As pretty as a butterfly,
As green as a snake,
As grizzly as a bear,
As pink as a bow,
As slimy as a snail.

Phoebe Milburn (8)
Holm Cultram Abbey CE Primary School, Abbeytown

Shark World

Shark World is...

As blue as the sky,
The sharks are as big as a house,
As wise as a tiger,
As fast as a speedy animal,
Teeth as sharp as a tiger,
A mouth as big as a bear.

Eddie Harrison (7)
Holm Cultram Abbey CE Primary School, Abbeytown

Welcome To The Glossy Sports Castle

The tall castle gates welcome the spectators in,
The ruined basketball net split unexpectedly as the fans drink,
Tall towers and heavy heads fill the castle walls,
Welcome to the Sports Castle!
Then, the luscious statues laugh like witches,
The vegetable fields grow appetizing food and have a rusted iron door,
The naughty neighbours try to break in like the FBI,
Welcome to the Sports Castle!
The secret door is as mysterious as a hyena,
The moon floats like an unusual torch,
The stairs creak and it was twenty-two feet down,
The poor cleaners stayed up all night to clean the forbidden area,
Welcome to the Sports Castle!

Daniel Petrov (9)
Our Lady & St Patrick's Catholic Primary School, Ewanrigg

The Mythical Underwater Castle

The castle gates whisper
As the mythical mermaids elegantly glide by,
The seahorse king as gold as the sun
Proudly counts his precious jewels,
The mindful guards carefully patrol the wonderland,
Sparkling castle, as the rainbow fish pass by,
The bell sings like an angel
As the dolphins' circle in pools,
Welcome to the mythical underwater castle!
Deep dark water, as cold as freezing ice,
Castle door whistles loudly as it creaks open,
Wide, sharp, spiky rocks roll on the seabed like dice,
Mystical animals of the sea all want to glide inside,
Welcome to the mythical underwater castle!

Rhiannan Brown (8)
Our Lady & St Patrick's Catholic Primary School, Ewanrigg

Magic Castle

Beautiful, magic unicorns sing like a peaceful angel in glorious Heaven,
The blue bubblegum door whispers hilarious jokes,
The sparkly, wise unicorn queen jumps on to the end
Of the glittery float that comes seventh,
Pink, fluffy candyfloss walls laugh as the fierce twin unicorns' horns broke,
Welcome to Magic Castle!
Blue fairies glide high in the sky,
Purple, scrumptious muffins sing a beautiful song,
The milk chocolate walls secretly hold a sneaky lie,
The red gummy heart windows shout at intruders as they walk by,
Welcome to Magic Castle!

Mya Johnson (9)
Our Lady & St Patrick's Catholic Primary School, Ewanrigg

The Lava Castle

The unsteady castle windows smash from the flash of the sun,
The lava spins like bike wheels
And the bridge screams like a ghost,
Most of the lava zombies are burning
From the suspicious sun as it shines on them,
The king's ten thousand zombies gather together as the king says his speech,
"Beware of the mighty castle!"
The lava zombies lined up to go on the diving board,
The doors begin to melt like ice cream,
The meat from the bakery smells like milk,
Beware of the mighty castle!

Matthew Anderson (9)
Our Lady & St Patrick's Catholic Primary School, Ewanrigg

Noah's Castle

The hectic ship is as tall as a tower,
The busy ship danced as the animals celebrated,
The adorable animals chuckled as the silky waves drifted past
Like a rain shower,
Magical light burst into the deep blue sky
As the party elevated,
The ship sang like the crazy animals dancing,
The stripy snake slithered around the lofty lighthouse,
As silly as a pirate,
The crazy crocodile dances,
Perky penguins paddle perfectly as the fun on the ship ends,
Welcome to Noah's Castle!

Ula (8)
Our Lady & St Patrick's Catholic Primary School, Ewanrigg

Noah's Ark

The hectic ship is as tall as a tower,
The busy ship danced as the animals celebrate,
The adorable animals chuckled as the silky waves drifted past like a rainbow,
Magical lights burst into the deep blue sky as the party elevated,
The lengthy green octopus shivered sneakily across the fragile sail,
The beautiful blue sky up high,
Dainty dog dithers as the wind curls around its tail,
Party over, animals sleep peacefully,
Was it good or was it a lie?
Welcome to Noah's Ark!

Nikita Clark (9)
Our Lady & St Patrick's Catholic Primary School, Ewanrigg

The Princess Castle

The princess' crown was as dazzling as the sun,
Villagers glided down the stunning rainbow slide,
Everybody shouts, "Fun! Fun! Fun!"
Magnificent rainbows are as powerful as a ride,
Welcome to Princess Castle!
The wealthy princess' beautiful blue eyes shine bright like a diamond,
Flowing hair glimmers as the pink streaks wave in the gentle breeze,
Everybody loves this place they call Rhyme Land,
A girl? A princess? A queen that may freeze,
Welcome to Princess Castle!

Miya Grace Goodwin (8)
Our Lady & St Patrick's Catholic Primary School, Ewanrigg

The Dreadful Fire Castle

Deadly Demon Castle shouts like an angry tiger,
Intruders break in but don't succeed,
Dreadful Fire King walks out and talks deeply to the guards,
Fire King made a deal with the intruders,
Welcome to the Dreadful Fire Castle.

Fire as deadly as a toxic python whale circles the castle walls,
The flammable turrets fire as intruders get tired,
Deadly Fire Guards shoot arrows as the demons laugh,
Deadly Fire King got tired, then got fired,
Welcome to the Dreadful Fire Castle!

Kenzie Riley (9)
Our Lady & St Patrick's Catholic Primary School, Ewanrigg

The Animal Party Ship

The hectic ship is as tall as a tower,
The busy ship danced as the animals celebrated,
The adorable animals chuckled as the silky waves drifted past,
Like a rain shower,
Magical lights burst in the deep blue sky
As the party elevated,
Animals sunbathe carefully
As the blazing sun heats the ship,
Joyful animals jump excitedly
Into the deep, turquoise sea
And take a tiny sip,
The ship sleeps silently, as do all the animals,
Except for the bee.

Niamh Margaret Herald (9)
Our Lady & St Patrick's Catholic Primary School, Ewanrigg

In The Flower Mansion

As the flowers sing to the perfect princess,
She falls asleep quietly,
Gazing out of the turrets at the spectacular view,
Fabulous flowers dance in the wind,
The castle is behind the bushes like a fox,

Welcome to the Flower Mansion!

Roses glisten beautifully in the sun,
Magically, she sees a sensational unicorn fly by,
Sleeping soundly after so much fun!
She wakes from a cry from the sky,

Welcome to the Flower Mansion!

Taylor Jardine (9)
Our Lady & St Patrick's Catholic Primary School, Ewanrigg

The Castle Of Galaxy

The gleaming, glooming castle laughs like a hyena,
Welcome to the Castle of Galaxy,
The moon gently lifts the castle up,
Welcome to the Castle of Galaxy!
The ancient castle gate leisurely howls
Like an elephant in the dark,
Welcome to the Castle of Galaxy!
The Galaxy king violently angers
Like an irritated lion,
Welcome to the Castle of Galaxy!
The undersea guards patrol the grounds
Like hungry sharks,
Welcome to the Castle of Galaxy!

Leighton Mcgarry (9)
Our Lady & St Patrick's Catholic Primary School, Ewanrigg

The Cake Castle

The rainbow bursts fill the colossal castle,
The huge castle is as strong as infinite bricks,
protecting them all,
Welcome to Cake Castle!
The white chocolate door
Sweet as a huge, white chocolate bunny that
sustains all,
Welcome to Cake Castle!
The guards that protect the cake castle
Are as strong as the Hulk!
Welcome to Cake Castle!
The turrets that shoot at the angry enemies
Trying to attack,
Welcome to Cake Castle!

Taylor Jack Dixon (8)
Our Lady & St Patrick's Catholic Primary School, Ewanrigg

The Maths Mountain

Welcome to Maths Mountain,
Where you will see an immense fountain,
You will hear the baffling bright boats belching brutally
And smell the wafting smell of food being cooked speedily,
Welcome to Maths Mountain!

Welcome to Maths Mountain,
A place where maths' signs enjoy bouncing
And mad mathematics announcing
The answers to puzzling sums which will make you go flouncing,
Welcome to Maths Mountain!

Oliver Kopec (9)
Our Lady & St Patrick's Catholic Primary School, Ewanrigg

The Water Castle Poem

The naughty guards try to take the king's special jewels,
Welcome to Undersea Castle!
The seahorse queen, as sparkly as glitter, carefully puts her treasure in her beautiful chest
In the underground kingdom,
The ground feels like it's covered with litter,
The bitter bread is delicious, like a blazing cupcake,
The weak castle gates shout
As the nice seashells sing beautifully,
Welcome to Undersea Castle!

Lexi-Jo Fearon (8)
Our Lady & St Patrick's Catholic Primary School, Ewanrigg

The Castle Of Fire

The turrets get annoyed as the window opens and shuts,
The long, wise towers watching down,
The windows stand generously as the lava looks on,
The turrets stare at the mighty crown,
This is the Castle of Fire!
Loudly, lava splashes around the bendy corners violently,
The gates are swishing up and down,
The doors bang aggressively,
The walls stand with a massive frown,
This is the Castle of Fire!

Kalan Burgess (9)
Our Lady & St Patrick's Catholic Primary School, Ewanrigg

The Undersea Castle

Under the sea, a glossy gold castle
Is as shiny as the sun,
The windows are as bright as the sky,
The guard's armour is as bright as gold,
The wall is as high as a tower,
Welcome to Undersea Castle!

The fish were as fast as lightning,
The king was counting his gold and diamonds,
The seahorse's swords were unbreakable,
Welcome to Undersea Castle!

Calvin Thompson (9)
Our Lady & St Patrick's Catholic Primary School, Ewanrigg

Animal Castle

All the animals peep out of petite windows,
The maids couldn't work and the chef couldn't cook,
Something was definitely amiss,
Welcome to Animal Castle!
Then, the lion rode the cat,
Meow!
And the frog croaks and the horse neighs,
The trumpet sang, the gates opened
And the guards stood,
The guards worked for the king.

Savanna Kirkbride (8)
Our Lady & St Patrick's Catholic Primary School, Ewanrigg

The Castle Of Animals

The unicorn and Pegasus neigh like angry horses,
Welcome to the animals' castle,
The castle walls whisper
Where the jewels are like spies,
Welcome to the animals' castle,
The shimmering sun shines like a glistening diamond,
Welcome to the animals' castle,
Cotton clouds skip through the air,
Welcome to the animals' castle!

Lexie Moore (8)
Our Lady & St Patrick's Catholic Primary School, Ewanrigg

Underwater Castle

Welcome to Underwater Castle,
The intimidating turrets make enemies run away,
The dolphins scatter to find the jewels for the King of the Sea,
The crabs go by, gliding through the castle,
The shells sing like villains in the castle pools,
Welcome to Underwater Castle!

Anthony Hine (9)
Our Lady & St Patrick's Catholic Primary School, Ewanrigg

The Castle On Fire

The gleaming red fire burns the unbreakable castle,
The gold, glistening turrets shine in the night light as the old crows fly by,
The moon levitates high in the sky as it cries,
The beaming clouds circle around the castle on fire,
Welcome to the Castle of Fire!

Jake Mcgarry (9)
Our Lady & St Patrick's Catholic Primary School, Ewanrigg

Chocolate Castle

Yummy chocolate bars bounce up and down on the rough wind,
The chocolate queen stares at the chocolate sky,
The melted chocolate curtains melt in the scorching sun,
The chocolate door sings like a beautiful angel,
Welcome to the Chocolate Castle!

Kianna Vollans (9)
Our Lady & St Patrick's Catholic Primary School, Ewanrigg

The Mythical Sea

Welcome to the Mythical Sea,
The pigmented turrets shine luminously,
Like the sun,
Welcome to the Mythical Sea!
The undersea castle shines, glistening like the blazing hot sun,
Welcome to the Mythical Sea!

Lexie Myers (8)
Our Lady & St Patrick's Catholic Primary School, Ewanrigg

The Underwater Art Session

Today, I had an art lesson,
It was a very long session,
It was at the bottom of the Atlantic
Where everyone is frantic,
There were kids having fun doing art
While they painted a heart,
There were lots of paints
That were very faint,
The paint was drying,
While kids were crying,
When it was bedtime,
They didn't go at the right time,
Instead, they played with slime,
Then, I went up to the top
To get a drink of pop.

Anna Sofia Bayles (9)
St Wilfrid's RC (VA) Primary School, Bishop Auckland

My Underwater Trampoline Park

Today, I went to the underwater trampoline park,
To see if I could see a great big shark,
My trampoline park is far away in the ocean,
Just like a big, big potion,
All around me, I could see,
People jumping, full of glee,
They could feel the air through their hair,
But they were chilling so they didn't care,
"Where are the sharks?" I began to wonder,
"Maybe they will come out when it starts to thunder?"

Hannah Maddison Snowball (9)
St Wilfrid's RC (VA) Primary School, Bishop Auckland

Today I Went To The Beach

Today, I went to the beach,
All I heard was a little bit of speech,
The speech came from an umbrella,
It was a cat acting like a fella,
All you could see was Titanic sinking,
People were jumping, leaping and thinking,
All I felt was soft sand upon my fingers,
All the rest made my hand linger,
I started to talk to a little turtle
And all he said was, "Have you seen my friend Murtle?"

Jack Bentley (9)
St Wilfrid's RC (VA) Primary School, Bishop Auckland

Unicorn Fashion Show

I saw a unicorn trotting down the lane,
In a gigantic, ancient blue plane,
Magic came out on a unicorn sun
Up in the sky, they had so much fun!
You could see all around, unicorns getting dressed,
They were trying to look their best,
Then, they started the show,
Then I started to blow,
At the end, Green Team won,
Everyone had so much fun!

Eva Ellourah Nottingham-Dennis (9)
St Wilfrid's RC (VA) Primary School, Bishop Auckland

Party Rainbow

I'm on a floating platform in the sky,
I hope I don't fall and die,
I'm on top of a floating rainbow,
I am bored, so I decide to sew,
I can see my dog jumping on clouds,
The dog is barking really loud,
I can feel Skittles on the rainbow,
I eat them like I'm on the go,
I get really, really sick
Whilst eating a lollipop stick!

Joshua Adam Cullen (8)
St Wilfrid's RC (VA) Primary School, Bishop Auckland

The Day I Surfed On The Sun

Today, I surfed on the sun,
You won't believe it was such great fun!
It was amazing on the sun,
I even found a cherry bun!
I felt like I was warming up like a chilli,
Careful, I might get silly,
When I surfed until noon,
I saw the North Star above the moon!
I decided to go for a break,
Maybe have some tea and cake!

Winnie Chasteauneuf (9)
St Wilfrid's RC (VA) Primary School, Bishop Auckland

Unicorn Fashion Show

Today, unicorns did a fashion show
While wearing sparkly hair bows,
High up in the tallest tree
The unicorns were having tea,
You could see a long stage,
But the long stage had a cage,
"I feel scared, I feel dizzy,
Why is my hair ever so frizzy?"
It didn't end so well
So they said, "Farewell!"

Tilly Jayne Ross (8)
St Wilfrid's RC (VA) Primary School, Bishop Auckland

The Day I Was On The Moon

Today, I am on the moon,
I floated here using a balloon,
I am up in the sky,
I really wanted to fly,
All I could see was floating rocks,
If it hit me, I would get an electric shock,
I was floating in the air
While I danced like I didn't care,
Then, I was feeling really sick,
So I began sitting a bit.

Charlie Fitzgerald (6)
St Wilfrid's RC (VA) Primary School, Bishop Auckland

Today I Went To Sea

Today, I saw a pool,
It was so cool,
It was in the sea,
Where a mermaid hurt her knee,
I touched a whale,
It started to chase its tail,
I swam with fish,
Hopefully, I'm not the shark's dish,
I swam to the top
To have some pop,
Nobody was there
Because there was a sea bear!

Ava May Race (8)
St Wilfrid's RC (VA) Primary School, Bishop Auckland

My Underwater Art Lession

Today, I had an art lesson
And it was a very long session,
It was in the sea where mermen lie
And steal each other's steak pie,
I saw lots of fish,
Which is my least favourite dish,
I could feel paint,
Which made me faint,
I swam back up to the top
To drink lots of pop!

Ellie Jane Sanders (9)
St Wilfrid's RC (VA) Primary School, Bishop Auckland

A Turtle Called Burtle

I met a talking turtle
And his name was Burtle,
I went to Los Angeles beach
And that was when he ate a peach,
The turtle got a dolphin ride
While they all tried to hide,
They could feel the sand
As it hit their hand,
As the turtle was talking loud
He began to draw a crowd.

Cody Andrew Mitchell (9)
St Wilfrid's RC (VA) Primary School, Bishop Auckland

All About Space

Today, I went to the planet Mars
And it was full of chocolate bars,
It was up in space
Because it was like a maze,
I felt like a hot bun
Because I was done!
It was lots of fun
Because it was done!
I saw holes in the planet Mars
Because it was like a chocolate bar!

Ella Turnbull (8)
St Wilfrid's RC (VA) Primary School, Bishop Auckland

The Day I Met Music

It was upside down in the air,
Wow, I was so high, I was scared,
There was a music lesson, that was cool,
In a flying swimming pool.
I saw the sun,
You won't believe it, I saw a bun!
I felt amazed
In front of my face,
Back to the ground
Safe and sound.

Adam Szabados (9)
St Wilfrid's RC (VA) Primary School, Bishop Auckland

Testing The Planets

Today, I went to Mars
Just to get some Milky Bars,
Today I went to Mars,
Just to look at the stars,
I felt a maze
In front of my face in space,
I saw the sun,
It looked like good fun,
I fell off a solar panel
While watching a TV channel.

Bradley Beau Wood (9)
St Wilfrid's RC (VA) Primary School, Bishop Auckland

I Hate My Job

My name is Bob
And I hate my job,
Working up in Mars
With chocolate bars,
With a giraffe that giggles,
While it poos out Skittles!
And burgers in the sky
That can fly way up high!
I wonder why I said it was bad,
I love my job, why was I sad?

Teddy Metcalfe (8)
St Wilfrid's RC (VA) Primary School, Bishop Auckland

In Out Of Space

Today, I went to space
To eat my own shoelace,
I started on Saturn
And danced a crazy pattern,
If I see a star
It might be my Granda
I'll need a spacesuit,
How will I eat fruit?
It was really fun,
I'm afraid my work is done!

Christopher Angell-Brown (9)
St Wilfrid's RC (VA) Primary School, Bishop Auckland

Shnogroogle

A Shnogroogle sport, all aliens play,
Something they do every day,
Coming from the cheese-like moon,
Just by using a wooden spoon.

With all of their alien power,
Flying higher every hour,
All aliens love this sport,
Even babies get taught!

Racing to touch freezing Mars,
They can zoom as fast as cars,
No balls are part of this game,
Racing to Mars is just their aim.

They do it at night, just in case
They might get caught doing their race,
They always play no matter what,
In icy cold or boiling hot.

Rubber ducks and flying kettles,
Weeds, flowers and stinging nettles,

They see it go by in a whizz!
Pots and pans go *bang! Fizz!*

The night goes by in a flash,
When it gets light, they have to dash,
A gold wooden spoon for the winner,
Then they fly back home for dinner.

Back up to their home called the moon,
Flying back on a wooden spoon,
Sparkling aliens of Kermit-frog-green,
Believe it or it won't be seen!

Holly Newman (10)
Teesside High School, Eaglescliffe

My Super Fabulous Candy Car

Oh, my super fabulous candy car,
My unique Wonderland candy car,
My roof is made of caramel,
My windows are made out of candy canes,
My seats are made out of crispy chocolate cake,
My wheels are made of delightful Oreo,
Oh, what a treat for children to meet,

All the children shout with smiles
And piles of excitement,
It's the super fabulous candy car!
It's on its way to Wonderland,
"Candy! Candy!" it shouts loudly,

The children's faces light up with delight
As they jump up with a joyful fright,
Oh, my candy car!
My fabulous super candy car!
What smiles it gives,
What joy it gives,

To the wonderful town of Wonders,
Sweets and treats galore!

Shayan Raja (8)
Teesside High School, Eaglescliffe

The Hungry Cactus

I saw a cactus running wild and free,
Minding his own business that I could see,
He bowed at the sand,
He bowed at the sky,
The next thing I know he's right next to me!

I jumped on the cactus,
Just waiting to scream.
But that didn't happen,
It just howled and bowed,
I looked at him and screamed, "Yeehaw!"
It sent me to speed as quick as a cheetah!

Finally, the cactus had put me down,
He looked so tired from running so long,
He looked so hungry from no water or food,
He looked at me with hope,
I didn't understand,
But the next thing I know
I'm all gobbled up!

Rohan Vagadia (11)
Teesside High School, Eaglescliffe

Welcome To Crazy England

I go to the fridge to get warm,
I sunbathe in a storm,
Sweets are very sour,
A minute is longer than an hour,
I walk on the sea
Yet swim on the land,
The sun comes out at night,
The moon shines all day bright,
I shower to keep dry,
I laugh when I cry,
Cats chase dogs,
I can see clearly in a fog,
I wear gloves on my feet
And socks on my hands,
Flowers grow from the sky, not the ground,
A penny is worth more than a pound,
This is crazy, upside down England,
Come and visit, take my hand (or foot!)

Amelia Mae Storey (11)
Teesside High School, Eaglescliffe

Candy Land

I could hear the delightful, mouth-watering
Sticky lollipop dancing and jumping
Down the chocolate river,
I could see candyfloss flying
Like fluffy clouds,
I could smell the sweet, sticky, crunchy popcorn
Filling the air with fun,
I could taste the yummy laces,
Yummy lollies, yummy chocolate frogs
And most of all, I could taste the yummy candy
corn,
I could feel the smooth, squishy jelly beans
And the multicoloured and fruity Skittles.

Natalie Hopkin (10)
Teesside High School, Eaglescliffe

My Mother's Perfume

I am so terribly thirsty,
I'm going to find a drink,
There is lots of fizzy pop
But also an aromatic stink.

Orange, cherry, lemon or cola?
I can't decide because of the pong,
There is an odd bottle up on the shelf
Giving a scent that's awfully strong!

I get myself a tall glass
And pick the odd bottle out of the gloom,
I pour a lot out into my glass,
My mum shouts, "No! My perfume!"

Layla Wild (11)
Teesside High School, Eaglescliffe

Flying Around The World On A Unicorn

We are flying high in the universe,
It feels magic,
My shiny, sparkly unicorn is lighting up the sky,
I can hear birds tweeting
And see children playing,
It's a magical feeling,
We are flying past the bright rainbow,
It's amazing,
I can see all the colours,
They are so bright,
We have passed America, Mexico
And now we are flying over Cuba,
This really is awesome,
I feel so lucky,
I have my own magical flying unicorn!

Roxi Hall (6)
Teesside High School, Eaglescliffe

The Hippogriff And The Yeti

I'm a friend of a Hippogriff
And we always holiday on Venus,
And me, myself,
I'm a magical monster too,
A Yeti who likes to play with the Hippogriff on Venus,
We can slug ice cream together while we swim in green jelly,
We chase each other for fun
And play pranks under the midnight sun,
My best trick was to drop my mouldy undershorts
On the Hippogriff's head!
It made him sneeze and turn bright red!

Gideon Kemp Green (7)
Teesside High School, Eaglescliffe

Rewinding Time

I rewound the time
And I felt just fine,
I found myself walking backwards
As the rain fell up
And the grass grew down,
I realised things may get awkward
As I went for my lunch,
I had a bit of a hunch
That things were going to get messy!
Out came my pudding, back into the dish,
Then out came my main course,
Chips and fish!
With a bit of shock
I reached for the clock
And reset the time correctly,
Phew!

Luke James Palmer (8)
Teesside High School, Eaglescliffe

My Special Award

I was in assembly one day,
When me and my friend
Were sneakily chatting away,
Suddenly, my name got a shout,
I thought I was going to get sent out.

Instead, I got sent up to the front,
But, surprisingly, I got a huge clap,
So then joined in Amy Blunt,
I was very proud
To get my name read aloud.

Then, I later found out
What it was about,
I was...
The best-behaved person in school!

Matilda Leader-Jenkins (10)
Teesside High School, Eaglescliffe

Swimming In My Cereal

I thought I must be swimming in my local swimming pool,
Until I saw some giant flakes floating all around,
I started with the doggy paddle and then I tried breaststroke,
But managed better on my back
Paddling through those flakes,
As I got to the other side
I felt like it was snowing,
The sticky, sweet snow rest on those crispy flakes,
The water I was swimming in turned cold and very white!

Esther Evie Anderson (8)
Teesside High School, Eaglescliffe

Lava Surfing

I dreamed of surfing on a volcano,
But I didn't know what to expect,
So I went to Mount Vesuvius
And took my surfboard along,
I climbed on top of my surfboard
And set off across the lava,
I was surfing, shouting, screaming,
I felt very hot indeed,
But it was still very exciting,
I was about to make history!
This wicked, mighty dream
Might just actually come true!

Ben Pumphrey (7)
Teesside High School, Eaglescliffe

I Had A Dream I Could Fly With My Pets

I was playing with my pets
When my dog grew wings,
My dog fluttered into the sky,
Then my hamster grew tiny wings
And drifted into the sky,
Next, my cat grew furry wings
And floated into the sky,
Suddenly, I grew wings,
All of us felt free, flying in the sky,
My dog, hamster and cat glided through the air,
When *crash!* My hamster, in fright, lost his hair!

Lucas Jones (8)
Teesside High School, Eaglescliffe

I Made A House Out Of Cookies

I made a house out of cookies,
It didn't go as planned...

The cookie crumbs stuck to my knees,
my face, my feet, my hands.
The chocolate chips melted all over the floor,
it was so sticky, I couldn't get to the door!
And I couldn't sleep in my bed
because the Smarties toppled down onto my head.
Ow! Ow! Ow!
I wish I hadn't done this now!

Amélie Evans de Launay (7)
Teesside High School, Eaglescliffe

Alice In Chocolate Land

Alice preferred Chocolate Land to Wonderland,
No crazy Queen or Cheshire Cat grinning,
Lucious, smooth chocolate for slurping,
Gushing rivers of Wispa swirling,
She munched her way through delicious treats,
Burping in delight before eating the sweets,
Lots of excitement was in the air,
But where was the Mad March Hare?
Back down the rabbit hole in Wonderland!

Beatrice Austin (10)
Teesside High School, Eaglescliffe

The Big Flying Dog

I had a ride on a big, flying dog,
We flew up so high to avoid the fog,
We flew past rivers and trees,
We were flying so fast we could feel the breeze,
I waved at a man flying a helicopter,
The blades were painted, metal copper,
We landed on the top of Roseberry Topping,
Then I said, "Goodbye!" to him so he could do his shopping!

Austin Stephen Eley (9)
Teesside High School, Eaglescliffe

Just Dogs

Big dogs, little dogs,
Many types of dogs,
Look after your animal friends,
Love and hug them lots.

Noisy dogs, quiet dogs,
Very, very friendly dogs,
Take them in the fields to play
And get muddy in bogs.

Silly dogs, crazy dogs,
Cute dogs and clever dogs,
Some dogs stand on two paws,
Beg, dance or are happy just to be dogs!

Luke Robinson (11)
Teesside High School, Eaglescliffe

Down The Rabbit Hole

Alice ate bread with mould
And low and behold, she caught a terrible cold,
She sneezed and sneezed and fell on her knees,
She felt like she couldn't breathe,
On her final sneeze
She fell into the trees
And down a rabbit hole
Where she found a mole,
They became best friends, 'til the very end,
Until Alice made a new friend.

Melissa Hopkin (10)
Teesside High School, Eaglescliffe

Tea Party On A Cloud

This year for my birthday,
I had a tea party on a cloud,
It was a very beautiful day
And the day was going my way,
We had a buffet for lunch,
With chocolate-filled cakes for dessert,
With rose-gold teapots, very fancy!
And there were birds singing overhead,
This birthday party was my best yet!

Isobel Pumphrey (10)
Teesside High School, Eaglescliffe

Football On The Moon

Wearing a spacesuit,
It's hard,
My helmet is heavy,
My feet feel weird,
Is that a moon man tackling me?
He's blue with big ears!
It's not fair!
He doesn't have to wear a heavy suit,
He's pinched the ball
And taken it down a crater!

Full-time!

Louis Main (9)
Teesside High School, Eaglescliffe

Flying

Once, I flew up to the clouds
And shouted aloud
As I started to play on my skateboard,
I whooshed and swooshed
Through the candyfloss sky
And did some fabulous tricks way up high,
It was soon time to go
So I whooshed down below
And landed in a bowl of chocolate,
Yummy!

Louisa Elizabeth Palmer (7)
Teesside High School, Eaglescliffe

The Planet

On the planet, it was dark,
But one day there was a light mark,
The mark shone bright, even at night,
The people were interested,
Soon they were tired, so they rested.

Felix Prince (6)
Teesside High School, Eaglescliffe

What To Do?

She closed the door
And said goodbye,
I let out an almighty sigh,
What should I do now?

Look out the window,
Where's she gone?
Now it's just me
With the radio on.

Suddenly, a knock at the door,
I opened it up and saw a paw,
To my surprise, it was the neighbour's cat,
Wearing nothing but a party hat!

"Come on over!" she said with a smile,
"Come to the party, it will last a while!"
As we crawled under the fence,
I couldn't stand the suspense.

Wow!

As we walked in the door,
I saw hamsters on the dancefloor,
What to do next?

I practised my moves
And got well into the decks,
Oops! Look at the time!

Quick, need to get home,
So she doesn't think I've been on the roam.

The key's in the lock
And it's nearly five o'clock,
I made it back,
As quick as a flash.

She opened the door,
I gave her my paw,
"Good boy!" she said,
Patting me on my head.

Amy Mitchell (11)
The Bishop Harvey Goodwin School, Carlisle

Olympics On The Silver Globe

When the first star lit in the moon sky,
All nations knew it was Olympics time,
On the silver globe
All the tickets were bought,
Moon Giraffe, Lion
And the crazy frog,

Crocodile Mile went silver diving first,
The craziest sport out of Planet Earth,
Mile said it was worth the nerve,
He went up and down and swirled all around.

Next up, Sally Snake, being the champion of dusty pong,
Before she started, she sang a song,
She made a ball out of the gloomy moondust,
She blew as hard as she could and always won!

Last, but not least, my favourite of all,
The upside down jelly was everyone's goal,

So many players but only one winner,
Last year's medalist was beaten by a beginner!

They all enjoyed it, the fans and players,
This years Olympics was better than ever!

Amelia Maria Per (11)

The Bishop Harvey Goodwin School, Carlisle

Fry Cheesy Moon Rocks

My trip to the moon did not go to plan...

Wandering happily through the sharp, grey
boulders on a warm, pretty day,
There's gooey, soft cheese gushing softly
Down a waterfall, splashing loudly,
Ooh, a moon rock! I thought joyfully,
"Big puddle!" I yelled,
The puddle was so bright, as bright as the sun
And a perfect golden yellow,
There was a wonderful scent swimming up my
nose,
Running happily through a pool of cheese,
Forgetting about the moon rock completely,
Thinking to myself, I suddenly remember the moon
rock,
It's got orange, squelchy stuff all over it,
It fell into a scalding, red-hot pool of lava,
The rock landed on metal,
The moon rock has been fried into bubbly cheese,
I ate it all up, "Yum! Yum!"

Chloe Watson (9)
The Bishop Harvey Goodwin School, Carlisle

My Adventure In Wonderland

It was a normal day, for what I could see,
It started with my sister reading to me.
She was in her glory
As she read me a story,
It became a long morning
As I thought it was boring.

So, I went for a walk
And came across a rabbit who could talk,
I followed him down a hole
That I always thought was there for a mole.

I followed him all the way down
And landed in a room full of brown.
At first look, I thought they were walls you see,
But, oh no, it's the ceiling, silly old me.

I then saw a cat who seemed rather strange,
I decided to follow him for a change.
Then, I met a queen who chopped off heads
And men made out of cards with a list full of dreads.

Lyla Nicholson (10)
The Bishop Harvey Goodwin School, Carlisle

Shrink To The Size Of An Ant

My walk through the woods didn't go to plan...

Jogging excitedly on a hot summer's day,
Cheerful birds quickly flying and loudly singing all around me,
Suddenly, a purple, shimmering potion came up before me,
As quick as a flash, I gulped it down,
All of a sudden, a cold shiver went down my spine,
I had become the size of an ant!
Suddenly, I found myself eating leaves,
They were not good,
I couldn't help it,
I went home to my mum to explain what had happened,
"Mum! Mum!" I shouted.
"Help! Help!" I screamed with all my might,
All of a sudden, I got stomped on!
Splat! On the floor.

Ellie Lindsley (9)
The Bishop Harvey Goodwin School, Carlisle

Riding On A Lightning Bolt

My trip to camp didn't go to plan...

Standing peacefully, waiting for the camp leader,
The wind muttered and a lightning bolt came,
It picked us up and *kaboom!*
The camp blew up and everyone was on the lightning bolt,
My socks came off,
We could see the whole place,
My parents and my friends let go but thankfully survived,
We took them to the Pokémon Centre,
But, before we could get there
The Blast Bolt (as I call it) took off again,
"Argh!" I said, angrily,
Finally, we made it home. I shouted, "Home!"

William Tuck (9)
The Bishop Harvey Goodwin School, Carlisle

Sunbathe On A Cloud

Sunbathing on a cloud did not go as planned...

Calmly sunbathing on a fluffy cloud, happily on a warm summer's day,
Merry birds tweeting loudly behind me,
As I sit on the cloud, I taste fresh air blowing in and out of my mouth,
I see birds flying gently by with their babies,
Fluffy clouds swishing around the sky while I bathe quietly,
I smell magnificent air soaring in the sky,
Suddenly, I wobble and I fall into my roof!
"Where have you been darling?" said Mother,
"You're grounded for a year!" said my dad,
"What!"

Nakita Carrigan (9)
The Bishop Harvey Goodwin School, Carlisle

If I Was A Dog

If I were my dog for a day,
I'd roll around and go out and play,
I'd chase the ball that went over the wall,
But I'd be sure to return on my owner's call,
I'd be right there, sat on his feet,
Waiting for those delicious treats,
But, wait, one moment, what's that I see?
A big black cat staring right at me!
With growling teeth and threatening eyes,
I shoot right from my owner's side,
Across the road and up the tree,
The cat has certainly got the better of me,
I guess that's just the dog's life for me!

Aden Swan (10)
The Bishop Harvey Goodwin School, Carlisle

Riding A Horse Through Space

My horse riding session didn't go as planned...

Standing excitedly in the middle of a field,
Heavy hooves clattering towards me,
I sat on my rainbow horse and felt its lovely skin,
It moved its hooves,
I could smell its hot breath,
Then, as quick as a flash,
It ran up the hill and into space,
I could feel the sun beaming against my skin,
I tasted the soft, sweet and fluffy clouds in my mouth,
Robots quickly zoomed past me,
The aliens on Mars were noisy,
Then, I fell down, back to the field,
Jumped off my horse and tumbled over!

Neve Todd (8)
The Bishop Harvey Goodwin School, Carlisle

The Queen's Coming To My House

The Queen's coming to my house!
The Queen's coming to my house!
Quick! Polish the glasses,
Quick! Hoover the stairs!
Don't burn the chicken
And fix that chair!

Quick Mum, the Queen's coming,
Quick Dad, fix that chair,
Mum, settle the baby
And Dad, fix that chair!

Kathleen, check the chicken
And *I'll* fix the chair,
Mum, settle the baby
And Dad, sit there!

Ahh, the Queen's here,
Nice and quiet,
Well, let's hope she likes that chair!

Keeley Brand (10)
The Bishop Harvey Goodwin School, Carlisle

Alice And The Wonderland

Alice, Alice, my good friend,
It's good to see you again,
With this warm, beautiful day,
Children playing in the day.

Did you drink that tasty drink
And turn so small, like a ring?
Did they tell that you were gone
And did you have fun?

With this tyre, would you play?
Hide-and-seek would you say?
Would you like to be the seeker?
But you can choose if you like!

With this warm and beautiful day,
We will play all day!
If you can't that's okay,
We will try another day!

Katie Bennett (10)
The Bishop Harvey Goodwin School, Carlisle

Vegetable Friends

Meet Percy Pea,
He's really very wee,
I found him at nursery,
He stays in my pocket,
Or sometimes in a locket,
I don't want to lose him you see,
He's chatty and funny
And worth lots of money,
Oh, I love Percy Pea!

Meet Candy Carrot,
I found her next to Percy,
I find them in my water whenever they are thirsty,
They make me laugh all day long
When they make fun of the turkey!
They'll be my friends forever
And ever,
I can't eat my little friends,
Never, never, never!

Ruby Vevers (11)
The Bishop Harvey Goodwin School, Carlisle

Aliens Say This, We Say That

Aliens say 'be bo' while we say English words,
Aliens say 'be', we say 'hi',
Aliens say 'bo', we say 'bye',
Aliens say 'beo', we say 'lie'.

Humans are different from aliens,
We sleep at night,
We learn at day,
Aliens sleep at dawn,
They hate the light,
Aliens say 'de tmogs', we say 'poems'.

As you see we are different to aliens,
I hope you now know how to speak alien,
'Cause you have no idea when you will see one!

Georgia Burns (11)
The Bishop Harvey Goodwin School, Carlisle

Camping

We packed our car, ready to go camping,
Although we would miss our home.
We went into the car, ready for our trip,
Hopefully, it wouldn't rain too much!
While on our way there, it was sunny,
But I thought that it would rain.
Dad tried to be funny,
But we just ignored him.
We unpacked our things and the tent,
Although it was only a small tent.
Mum wanted to go for a walk,
But I missed the WiFi in the house.
The next day, we went for a walk,
But it rained as soon as we got lost!

Kieran Oliver Wilson (11)
The Bishop Harvey Goodwin School, Carlisle

Skip On A Rocket

My blast-off didn't go as planned...

Exploring the moon, I saw an alien on a rocket ship,
People were talking anxiously about an unknown artefact,
The alien skipped up and down the rocket
While the other guys were talking loudly inside the rocket,
I was looking at the alien, shocked,
Through the space window, there was a mean, scary alien,
When I was done, I went to eat some space food,
The aliens came in the space kitchen,
We ran away, we were terrified,
I had to jump out of the window!

Jacob Duncan (8)
The Bishop Harvey Goodwin School, Carlisle

Shrink To The Size Of An Ant

My summer stroll didn't go as planned...

Strolling quickly around the bright grassy hill during a heatwave,
Tall grass was rustling all around me,
Accidentally, I tripped over and skidded across the floor into a wavy bush,
A familiar, disturbing smell entered my nostrils,
Worryingly, I swallowed a horrible leaf,
Unexpectedly, I felt I was shrinking as fast as a cheetah could run,
Unluckily, I was getting smaller, smaller and smaller until...
I'd shrunk to the size of an ant!

Ryan Wilson (9)
The Bishop Harvey Goodwin School, Carlisle

Shrink To The Size Of A Puppy

My stroll around the grassy hill didn't go as planned...

Strolling quickly around the bright grassy hill during a heatwave,
Tall grass was rustling around me,
Accidentally, I tripped over and skidded across the floor into a wavy, giant bush,
A familiar, disgusting smell entered my nostrils,
Worryingly, I swallowed a horrible leaf,
Unexpectedly, I felt I was shrinking as fast as a cheetah could run,
Unluckily, I had gotten smaller, smaller,
I'd shrunk to the size of a puppy!

Harvey Richardson (8)
The Bishop Harvey Goodwin School, Carlisle

Make A House Of Crisps

My camping trip didn't go as planned...

Quietly looking around on a gloomy day,
This is a horrible day,
Exploring the forest for treasure,
Merry birds tweeting behind me,
Slowly, I was still walking,
Suddenly, I thought I heard something,
But it was nothing, it was just the tree,
Then, I found a friend,
We were walking together,
Suddenly, we found a treasure chest with bags of crisps,
I ran to my family,
We started building a house out of crisps!

Daniel Walker (9)
The Bishop Harvey Goodwin School, Carlisle

Shrink To The Size Of An Ant

My trip to the haunted house didn't go as planned...

Walking urgently through the haunted house,
In the distance, people were gathering together urgently,
There was a strange smell in the other room,
Walking into the room, I found a potion,
I tasted the potion
And it shrunk me to the size of an ant!
When I was so, so, so little,
I saw a monstrous, enormous spider!
He looked at me and started to chase me,
When the spider caught me, he started eating me!

Olivia Aurelia Per (9)
The Bishop Harvey Goodwin School, Carlisle

Lick A Shark

My trip to the zoo didn't go as planned...

Exploring the zoo excitedly,
Many sharks splashing loudly behind me,
I slipped into the shark pool quickly,
I tried to lick the shark but it swam away,
It looked like a hairy shark,
I licked the shark when it calmed down,
It tasted of horrible hair,
I was scared that I would get eaten,
The terrifying shark's mouth opened wide and gobbled me up!

Brandon (8)
The Bishop Harvey Goodwin School, Carlisle

Cookie Moon

Once, I saw a cookie moon,
I couldn't believe it myself,
The last time I saw cookies
They were on my mother's shelf!
You might think that it's a myth,
But I can promise you this,
This is definitely not a myth,
And the cookie moon tastes like bliss,
The cookie moon was made of dough
And lots of chocolate chips,
The thought that I could eat it all
Made me lick my lips.

Charley Read (8)
The Bishop Harvey Goodwin School, Carlisle

Ride A Lightning Bolt

My camping trip didn't go to plan...

Rushing quickly through the camp,
Heavy lightning striking the ground,
Suddenly, one of the bits of lightning bolt hit me,
I could taste cold, bitter curry,
I could smell the vile rubble,
I could feel the scorching heat of the lightning bolt,
Could this really be happening?
Suddenly, I climbed on the lightning bolt and flew into space.

Alfie Michael Burke (8)
The Bishop Harvey Goodwin School, Carlisle

Shrink To The Size Of An Ant

My trip to the haunted house did not go to plan...

Walking happily through the haunted house,
People gathering around in a crowd,
The smell of a potion,
I drank it and turned into an ant!
Suddenly, I saw a man walking into the house,
He stepped on me!
I was as flat as a pancake,
He broke my left foot,
As I heard the door banging on the gate.

Alfie Sims (9)
The Bishop Harvey Goodwin School, Carlisle

Outer Space Football Match

I once had an idea to play football in space,
I told a few friends who just laughed in my face,
I built a big rocket from boxes and cans
To transport the players and the dedicated fans,
We all counted down, ready to go,
Some feared the worst, is she gonna blow?
Within a split second, we shot in the air,
Boldly going to play football where no one else dared!

Aimee Porter (11)
The Bishop Harvey Goodwin School, Carlisle

Cookie Planet

Everything is cookies on Cookie Planet,
Even the trees are made of cookies,
The ground, although biscuity, is hard as granite,
People of Cookie Planet are a mixture of all sorts,
Some are chunky,
Some are thin
And some are a mixture of light and dark
chocolate,
They love all sports,
I hope you visit soon,
Just don't bring a spoon!

Lewis Mitchell (11)
The Bishop Harvey Goodwin School, Carlisle

Underwater BBQ

My underwater BBQ didn't go to plan...

Playing, full of excitement,
I was under the sea, exploring,
Fish blew bubbles all around me,
Disgusting, cold seaweed was in the kebabs,
Horrible fish were in my burger,
Soggy, squishy sharks were surrounding me quietly,
I hated it so much!

Nakita Currie (9)
The Bishop Harvey Goodwin School, Carlisle

Sew The Scales To A Mermaid's Tail

My trip to the ocean didn't go to plan...

I saw a dangerous shark,
I ate my picnic,
I saw a mermaid with a long tail,
She said, "Please help me sew on my shiny, rainbow pearl scales?"
I began to sew them on,
"Oh no! There's not enough!
What shall I do?"

Latiesha Smith (9)
The Bishop Harvey Goodwin School, Carlisle

The Wolf

We growl and snarl and pounce on prey,
But first, we follow tracks.
We follow you when you are sleeping
With hypnotising packs.
We search, we lurk with yellow eyes and
At a full moon, we whisper this tune,
The wolf,
The wolf,
The wolf!

Liam Connor (11)
The Bishop Harvey Goodwin School, Carlisle

I Like Cats Because...

I like cats because...
Sometimes they are chaotic,
Sometimes they are funny,
Sometimes they are five colours,
Sometimes they are four colours,
But who cares anyway?
I like them all!

Kyle Blythe (10)
The Bishop Harvey Goodwin School, Carlisle

Sausage In The Air

My dinner started to float off!
My sausage was in the air,
The beans followed,
The sauce flew off,
The spoons swirled around
And the mash landed in my face!

Tyler Harris Michael (10)
The Bishop Harvey Goodwin School, Carlisle

Food Zombie

Shaun saw a zombie,
He was eating a glombie,
"You're going to be sick,
I'll have to be quick,
I'll run and get some rotten tics
That will make you very sick!"

Shaun Moran (10)
Villa Real School, Villa Real

Baa Baa Green Goat

Baa baa green goat,
Have you any oats?
Yes man, yes man
Three times four,
One for the llama,
One for the man
And one for the little fox
Who lived in a can.

Flynn Elliott John Norton (11)
Villa Real School, Villa Real

Bendy And The Ink Machine

Bendy and the ink machine,
Ate his supper with a gene,
He played his Super Mario game
And broke it, what a shame!
He went to buy a new one
And it was just the same.

Aiden Thomson (8)
Villa Real School, Villa Real

The Gribble

Once, there was a gribble,
He had a little dribble,
At night he was asleep
And he was snuggling with a sheep!

Nathaneal Williams (11)
Villa Real School, Villa Real

The Cow That Went Kaboom

The cow that went kaboom!
Ended up on the moon,
He didn't know where to go,
So he wiggled his big toe,
That took him to Mars,
There, he ate all the stars
And when he was full,
He gave his tail a pull,
That took him to Jupiter,
Where he only got stupider,
He jumped up and down
As if he was a clown!
He swirled and swooped in some kind of dream,
Then he landed somewhere and thought of a scheme,
"I will look for a map and find my way home!"
But that all went wrong because of a gnome,
The gnome was small and liked to snort,
He tried to catch him, but he couldn't be caught,

He tried to look sad, but that all backfired,
So instead, he gave up because he was lonely and tired,
"I must get home but I don't know how!"

Scarlett Anne Chambers (10)
Warcop CE Primary School, Warcop

Kitty's On The Loose

Kitty's on the loose,
She's like a wild goose,
We're on a chase,
Where is the place?
Get in the car!

Kitty's in a tree!
Quick, get a ladder,
If we don't she will get sadder!

Kitty's down now,
She's safe and sound.

Oh no! She's on the run,
To tell the truth, it isn't much fun,
Got her in my arms!

Again? She's run away on a raft,
Well, she is kind of daft,
I hopped on too and hugged her tight.

I just realised where we are,
We've actually travelled quite far!

Abbie Heron (9)
Warcop CE Primary School, Warcop

The Secret Little Land

One little stroke of a dachshund,
Boom! I disappeared, into a land,
On the outside, it looked like a cloud,
But on the inside, it is something completely different,
Dachshund Land!
I was the first person to ever enter it.

The dachshunds were wearing clothes just like humans,
They also had a swimming pool and a shopping centre,
The cloud smelled of Smarties,
The strangest part was this...
The dachshunds ate human food and for a treat, dog food!

I now know a secret little land
Full of dachshunds!

Grace Featherstone (9)
Warcop CE Primary School, Warcop

Super Cat

Once, there was a cat who was really fat,
He liked food,
Then, one day, his owners dropped a bar of plutonium
In the gloop, as the cat ate it,
Suddenly, he went swoosh and swish and shot up in the air,
He flew over the city,
Looking with pity
And swooped down to get a closer look,
Then he saw a robber was starting to slobber,
So he put him in jail
Without fail
And flew into the sky,
As he flew through the city, people yelled,
"Is it a bird?
Is it a plane?
No, it's a cat!"

Jenson Schug (8)
Warcop CE Primary School, Warcop

Mr Hutchinson

My old teacher, Mr Hutchinson,
Is as old as a tree,
He always needs the toilet,
I need a wee!

My old teacher, Mr H
Is as funny as cheese,
But whenever he goes to lunch
He never eats his peas.

My old teacher, Mr H
Is as strict as a mad kitten,
He doesn't look like one,
In fact, you can call him a mitten.

My old teacher, Mr H
Is also very scary
And here he comes,
He is also very wary.

This is the story of Mr H.

Alexander Fok Sheng Yi (10)
Warcop CE Primary School, Warcop

The Queen's Underwear!

As everyone knows,
The Queen has
Just a couple of thousand
Pairs of underpants!

They're big, they're small,
Wide and tall,
Short and thin,
She probably hasn't worn them all!

They feel rough, fluffy, rubbery,
Silky and scaly.

They're red, they're blue,
Orange, yellow, green,
Spotty, stripy, polka dot pink,
Lovehearts and stars!

None are the same,
All are unique!

Tabitha Paul (9)
Warcop CE Primary School, Warcop

Lava And TNT

What fun is there in normal surfing?
Water and wood,
That isn't so good,
Lava and TNT, now that sounds like me!
So off I go to an erupting volcano,
To try what I have seen,
At the top I'm about to go off,
The lava is hurting my feet,
Down I go through the lava, oh!
There's fire coming from my knees!
My hair is alight, oh, what a fright!
There's only a skeleton left of me!

Hannah Eife (9)
Warcop CE Primary School, Warcop

Volcano

I was in a volcano with a cookie,
The lava floated up and down,
Suddenly, it went pop!
When I was sat on a rock!
I quickly jumped off,
Grabbed my pet cookie
And burst down the rock,
I realised it wasn't lava,
It was tonnes of cookie!
I stopped and I ate one,
This turned me into a cookie,
I was scared!
But then, a hand picked me up
And dropped me,
I was back to normal!

Yanic Peter Voican (8)
Warcop CE Primary School, Warcop

A Unicorn On An Alien Ship

Down by the water, down by the water,
I got pulled in and I shouted for my daughter,
Up behind I came to find unicorns on the headline,
Down below I came to see
Upside down houses floating up above me,
Then came down a unicorn in a saucer,
Then I thought, *is he dumb?*
Where will I go? Where will I go?
Something is happening to me,
Where will I go? Where will I go?

Charlotte Smith (9)
Warcop CE Primary School, Warcop

The Table Who Ate Humans

Did you know that tables ate humans?
Well, now you know they did!
The last one that tried to attack me
Was half the size of me,
They would eat the vet and the doctor,
They were very fat and hungry,
They would eat a load of humans,
They would even eat our favourite teacher,
They never stopped eating,
Once, I even saw one running on its big metal legs!

Lacey Kelly (10)
Warcop CE Primary School, Warcop

In Wonderland

I wonder what lies high in the sky.
Do fairies fly? Why do they fly? Do they have homes?
Imagine portals big, high and small!
Elves scamper in the wood,
The winter sugar snow falls down
As if it is shaken in a sieve,
The trees are lollipops,
Lick them, they taste delicious!
The king, he is part squirrel, cat and penguin,
How different is he?

Robyn Cartwright (9)
Warcop CE Primary School, Warcop

The Evil Golf Ball

One day on the golf course in Appleby,
There was an evil golf ball
And a nice golf ball
Who ate people,
The evil one ate Bob the slob,
So Bob the slob became evil
And the kind ball ate John Daly,
John Daly struck Bob the slob
With a piece of wood on the head
In the rough grass,
The good ball smirked
And hopped away,
Yay!

Corey Tallentine (9)
Warcop CE Primary School, Warcop

Donkey Sat On A Chair

Donkey, donkey sat on a rat,
Donkey, donkey sat on a cat,
Donkey, donkey sat on a mat,
Donkey, donkey sat on a chair.

Donkey, donkey sat on a stool,
Then the donkey made a fool
By jumping in the pool,
He whacked a stool and found a mule,
He found his house and went to type,
Then donkey went home to sleep.

Toby Bowness (10)
Warcop CE Primary School, Warcop

The Cow That Went Pow!

I know a cow that went *pow!*
It lived at Jellyton Farm,
It crackled and crackled until, at last,
In a blast, it exploded
Making the most terrible noise,
It went *pow!*
It went *pop!*
It went *kapow!*
And it went *kapop!*
I know a cow that went *pow!*

Tilda Bell (9)
Warcop CE Primary School, Warcop

SGT Boxers Vs Laughing Knickers

Everyone remembers the
Battle of Underpants,
One army led by SGT Boxers
Versus the Laughing Knickers.
The Underpants army got in their pants spaceship
And loaded it with tanks that shot underwear balls
And they flew to Planet Cheesier,
Which is Burger Jupiter,
And the war started...

Hugo Fennell (8)
Warcop CE Primary School, Warcop

The Evil Chihuahua

The evil Chihuahua monster is a horrible creature,
It has demon eyes, gigantic legs and sharp teeth,
I could smell the horrible Chihuahua,
I could see the destruction,
I could taste the air of the Chihuahua,
The evil Chihuahua is a horrible creature,
It still lives to this day!

Rohan Knowles (9)
Warcop CE Primary School, Warcop

The Flipping Sheep Timmy

Once, there was a sheep,
A really silly sheep
Who was called Timmy,
The flipping sheep Timmy,
He flipped a lot,
And one day he flipped into a rocket
Called Barshalooshapoosh,
The rocket could jump,
Climb, drink and eat,
And Timmy lived in the rocket, flipping.

Scarlett Joan Brass (9)
Warcop CE Primary School, Warcop

Shadow Santa

Santa, oh, Santa, what have you done?
What a situation, what have you done?
Ruining Christmas for the boys and girls,
What have you done?
Destroying their spirit, what have you done?
Ruining their spirits has taken away yours,
The negative is a shadow, what have you done?

Olly Frederick Hughes (8)
Warcop CE Primary School, Warcop

I Have A Cat

I have a cat,
It goes splat!
She flies in the wind
And slides on the ice,
Fluffy unicorns she loves,
Like pink and orange doves,
Exploding rainbows in the air,
All around, just like a dare,
Hair, oh hair!
It's everywhere!
Why?
I have a cat.

Arianna Kayla Voican (9)
Warcop CE Primary School, Warcop

The Menacing Teacher

The menacing teacher
Is a scary book eater,
As I walked in
I could taste his anger,
I could smell the smoke from the classroom,
I could feel the madness,
I could see the wreck of the classroom,
Maybe I will go to Mrs Framer's class instead...

Lois Dinsdale (8)
Warcop CE Primary School, Warcop

I Went Parachuting Underwater

I went parachuting underwater,
A shark started racing around,
Then some man-eating fish started surrounding me,
When I started to get scared,
The seaweed started to tickle my feet,
I was too busy laughing
To realise the shark was coming towards me!

Arthur Dow (8)
Warcop CE Primary School, Warcop

100 Pieces Of Dynamite

I was riding on an aeroplane,
I got caught on a shark,
I came plummetting down,
I saw dynamite on the back.

I was worried,
I was scared,
I jumped off the shark to the sea below,
The shark landed in the volcano
Which erupted!

Rory Hewetson (8)
Warcop CE Primary School, Warcop

Lick A Shark

One day, I licked a shark in a volcano,
When I licked the shark, it swam off,
I saw an alien drinking,
The alien was drinking the shrimp food
But then it drank him!
Suddenly, I felt a shake,
Oh my, it was the shark!
It was back!

Harry Scott Lofthouse (8)
Warcop CE Primary School, Warcop

A Sausage Dog Ate Donald Trump

In 2121, sausage dogs took over.
They were so smooth and cute,
Donald Trump went to stroke one,
It opened its mouth but didn't bark.
It let out a tremendous noise
And swallowed Donald Trump in one,
After that, it only burped!

Max Maltby (8)
Warcop CE Primary School, Warcop

YoungWriters
Est. 1991

Young Writers Information

We hope you have enjoyed reading this book – and that you will continue to in the coming years.

If you're a young writer who enjoys reading and creative writing, or the parent of an enthusiastic poet or story writer, do visit our website **www.youngwriters.co.uk**. Here you will find free competitions, workshops and games, as well as recommended reads, a poetry glossary and our blog. There's lots to keep budding writers motivated to write!

If you would like to order further copies of this book, or any of our other titles, then please give us a call or visit **www.youngwriters.co.uk**.

Young Writers
Remus House
Coltsfoot Drive
Peterborough
PE2 9BF
(01733) 890066
info@youngwriters.co.uk

Join in the conversation!
Tips, news, giveaways and much more!

YoungWritersUK   @YoungWritersCW